From the Bible-Teaching

CHARLES R. S

D0199061

Cultivating
PURITY
in an
IMPURE
World

LifeMaps

Insight for Living

CULTIVATING PURITY IN AN IMPURE WORLD
A LIFEMAPS BOOK

From the Bible-Teaching Ministry of Charles R. Swindoll

Charles R. Swindoll has devoted his life to the clear, practical teaching and application of God's Word and His grace. A pastor at heart, Chuck has served as senior pastor to congregations in Texas, Massachusetts, and California. He currently pastors Stonebriar Community Church in Frisco, Texas, but Chuck's listening audience extends far beyond a local church body. As a leading program in Christian broadcasting, *Insight for Living* airs in major Christian radio markets around the world, reaching people groups in languages they can understand. Chuck's extensive writing ministry has also served the body of Christ worldwide and his leadership as president and now chancellor of Dallas Theological Seminary has helped prepare and equip a new generation for ministry. Chuck and Cynthia, his partner in life and ministry, have four grown children and ten grandchildren.

Published by IFL Publishing House, a division of Insight for Living
Post Office Box 251007, Plano, Texas 75025-1007

Based upon the original outlines, charts, and transcripts of Charles R. Swindoll's sermons, *Cultivating Purity in an Impure World* was collaboratively developed by the Creative Ministries Department of Insight for Living.

Editor in Chief: Cynthia Swindoll, President, Insight for Living
Director: Mark Gaither, Th.M., Dallas Theological Seminary
Writer: Wayne Stiles, Th.M., D.Min., Dallas Theological Seminary
Theological Editor: Michael J. Svigel, Th.M., Dallas Theological Seminary
Content Editor: Amy Snedaker, B.A., English, Rhodes College
Copy Editors: Brie Engeler, B.A., University Scholars, Baylor University
Cari Harris, B.A., Journalism, Grand Canyon University
Mike Penn, B.A., Journalism, University of Oklahoma
Designer: Joe Casas, Graphic Design, Attended the University of North Texas
Production Artist: Nancy Gallaher, B.F.A., Advertising Art, University of North Texas

ISBN 1-57972-536-8
Printed in the United States of America

Table of Contents

A Letter from Chuck

"Christianity is supremely the champion of purity."

Those words seemed to spring off the page of a book I read some years ago. Theoretically, of course, it's true. There *is* no power like the power of Jesus Christ to make a man or woman pure. But that power is not automatic.

I saw the reality of those words up close and personal almost fifty years ago after I headed overseas to serve in the Marines. Before I ever dropped the seabag off my shoulder, I faced a decision. I was going to have to live in a barracks full of godless lifestyles. Surrounded by men who couldn't have cared less about the things of God, away from my home and wife and family and all of my accountability, I was just a nameless face on the streets of Okinawa thousands of miles from anyone who knew me. The decision I made that first day to remain pure was tested every single day of those sixteen months. By the grace of God alone, He provided a way of escape each time I faced temptation. But it wasn't easy.

The same year I completed my military service and was honorably discharged, the book I quoted above was published. I can't help relate the quote to my experience: "Christianity is supremely the champion of purity." Without God, remaining morally pure would have been impossible.

We've come a long way in the last five decades. And yet some things never change. We live in an impure world. Yet God still calls us to cultivate purity.

In more than forty years of ministry I have seen the fierce battle for sexual purity take its toll on many lives, including several fellow ministers. But I can attest from personal experience, as well as from the lives of many others, that the battle is winnable with God. That's the hope-filled message of this book!

I'm thrilled to contribute to such a significant series as *LifeMaps*. The first volume you hold in your hands speaks to one of the most urgent needs of our day.

I'm confident that if you will commit yourself to applying the chapters we've crafted, you will enjoy a freedom perhaps like you've never known before—a freedom God has provided for you.

We *can* live a pure life—even in an impure world.

Let's continue that journey together,

Charles R. Swindoll

At its heart, a map is the distillation of the experience of travelers——those who have journeyed in the past and recorded their memories in the form of pictures and symbols. The map represents the cumulative wisdom of generations of travelers, put together for the benefit of those now wishing to make that same journey.

To undertake a journey with a map is therefore to rely on the wisdom of the past. It is to benefit from the hard-won knowledge of those who have explored the unknown and braved danger in order to serve those who will follow in their footsteps. Behind the lines and symbols of the map lie countless personal stories——stories the map itself can never tell. Yet sometimes those stories need to be told, just as the hard-won insights of coping with traveling can encourage, inspire, and assist us.[1]

——Alister E. McGrath

Welcome to *LifeMaps*

On a journey, the important thing is not speed as much as it is *direction*.

But sometimes heading the right way requires some guidance. Think about it. You would never set out on a long road-trip without first making sure you knew which direction to go, right? You'd consult a map. For many people, the journey toward a deeper and more meaningful relationship with God lies along new or unfamiliar ground. They need directions; they need a map. And, even with a map, sometimes you can still get lost. When you do, it's the locals who know best—those who have been down the same roads. That's why this book is designed to be completed in concert with someone else. Wise friends or counselors can encourage us in our spiritual growth and help us avoid pitfalls along our paths.

Using *LifeMaps*

LifeMaps provides opportunities for individuals to interact with the Bible in different settings and on several levels, depending upon your particular needs or interests. *LifeMaps* also places a tool in the hands of pastors and other Christian leaders, helping them guide others along a journey of spiritual growth through the study and application of the Bible.

For Individuals

You can use *LifeMaps* in your personal devotions to gain God's perspective on a particular area of Christian living. In addition to offering engaging chapters to read, *LifeMaps* can further your journey of spiritual growth with the help of penetrating questions and opportunities for personal application.

LifeMaps can also serve as a first step to healing or resolving an issue that continues to plague you. Read, reflect, answer the questions, and then contact a competent, mature, godly man or woman to discuss the topic as it relates to your personal situation. This individual can be a pastor, a counselor, or even one of our staff here at Insight for Living in the Pastoral Ministries Department. See page 101 for information on how to contact Insight for Living. This step is an essential part of the journey.

For Pastors and Counselors

LifeMaps is designed to guide individuals through an engaging, in-depth study of the Word of God, freeing you to help them apply the truths in even more specific and personal ways. As a vital first step in the counseling process, each volume lays a solid biblical, theological, and practical foundation upon which you can build. Encouraging individuals to work through the book on their own allows them the time necessary for personal reflection and education while enabling you to target your ministry of personal interaction, discipleship, and accountability to their particular needs.

For Groups

LifeMaps can serve as a curriculum for home Bible studies, Sunday school classes, and accountability or discipleship groups. Though intensely personal in application, each book in the series contains enough material for group discussion of key questions and noteworthy passages. *LifeMaps* can also foster meaningful interaction for pastors, elders, staff, and Christian leaders during staff devotionals, leadership retreats, or board meetings.

Jonathan Edwards, perhaps America's most influential and forward-thinking theologian, wrote this about the value of groups in our Christian pilgrimage:

> Let Christians help one another in going this journey.
>
> —There are many ways whereby Christians might greatly forward one another in their way to heaven, as by religious conference, etc. Therefore let them be exhorted to go this journey as it were in company: conversing together, and assisting one another. Company is very desirable in a journey, but in none so much as this.
>
> —Let them go united and not fall out by the way, which would be to hinder one another, but use all means they can to help each other up the hill.
>
> —This would ensure a more successful traveling and a more joyful meeting at their Father's house in glory.[1]

Suggestions for Study

Whether you use *LifeMaps* in a group, in a counseling setting, in the classroom, or for personal study, we trust it will prove to be an invaluable guide as you seek deeper intimacy with God and growth in godliness.

In any setting, the following suggestions will make *LifeMaps* more beneficial for you.

- Begin each lesson with prayer, asking God to teach you through His Word and to open your heart to the self-discovery afforded by the questions and text.

- Read the chapters by Chuck with pen in hand. Underline any thoughts, quotes, or verses that stand out to you. Use the pages provided at the end of each section to record any questions you may have, especially if you plan to meet with a pastor or counselor.

- Have your Bible handy. Following each chapter by Chuck, you'll be prompted to read relevant sections of Scripture and answer questions related to the topic.

- As you complete each lesson, close with prayer, asking God to apply the wisdom and principles to your life by His Holy Spirit. Then watch God work! He may bring people and experiences into your life that will challenge your attitudes and actions. You may gain new insight about the world and your faith. You may find yourself applying this new wisdom in ways you never expected.

May God's Word illumine your path as you continue your journey. We trust that this volume in the *LifeMaps* series will be a trustworthy guide to learning and to your spiritual growth.

Cultivating
PURITY
in an
IMPURE
World

Chapter I

How the Mighty Have Fallen

The shrill ring of the telephone broke the silence in my study. The caller's message broke my heart. Another fellow minister had fallen morally. Another soldier of the cross who once stood tall—who had armed his congregation with truth and encouraged them to stand strong against the adversary—had disgracefully deserted the ranks and given victory to the enemy by his sin. Even before I put the receiver down, tears flooded my eyes.

An ancient scene flashed through my mind. A sickening scene. A battlefield in Israel called Mount Gilboa, littered with the bodies of Hebrew soldiers after a tragic day of combat against the Philistines. Among the dead lay a tall, seasoned warrior king named Saul. How the pagans of Philistia must have gloated in their victory over the army of God!

Even though Saul had turned David's life into a nightmare for more than a dozen years, David lamented the king's death with the words, *Ache naph-lu gi-boreem b'thoke hameel chamah*. Which, being translated, expressed his anguish, "How the mighty are fallen in battle."

As I sat alone in my study, I wondered if that line came back to haunt David twenty years later. "How the mighty are fallen." In the passing of two decades David has become fifty years of age; the middle-aged years of prosperity and favor. He has by now not only succeeded Saul, he's taken Israel to new heights. Never once has David experienced defeat on the battlefield. Some estimate that his brilliant military campaigns and wise, visionary leadership expanded Israel's land area over ten times its original size. Rival armies shuddered at the thought of invading Israel. David gave the nation a flag to fly—the Star of David waved over the country as Hebrew citizens swelled with national pride. Israel's commerce thrived as caravan routes expanded into new areas, bringing enormous wealth into the treasury. And the cream of this astounding prosperity poured into David's cup so that by the time he reached his fifties, he enjoyed the luxury of a brand new place of residence called "the King's Palace." All the while, he set aside money and materials to build a temple in honor of his God.

David's name had become a household word all across Israel. Foreign kings envied his success and fame. In that day, everyone had heard of David. G. Frederick Owen wrote,

> The Arameans and the Amalekites
> were in turn conquered. Commercial
> highways were thrown open and in
> came merchandise, culture, and wealth
> from Phoenicia, Damascus, Assyria,
> Arabia, Egypt and more distant lands.
> To his people David was king, judge and
> general, but to the nations round about,

he was the leading power in all the Near
Eastern World—the mightiest monarch
of the day.[1]

No leader stood taller than David, "The Mighty."

Then came the day he saw Bathsheba. God preserved the story of this good man's moral collapse in
2 Samuel 11:1–5 for the benefit of all who would come
after him. But before we cut into his failure, before we
begin the autopsy on David's moral fall, let me offer a
word of caution. This chapter is not merely the retelling
of one man's failure. It's not an occasion to cluck our
tongues and wag our heads. It's a message to all of
us. First Corinthians 10:12 says it best, "Let him who
thinks he stands take heed lest he fall" (NKJV).

An Autopsy of a Moral Fall

Look closer. Sandwiched between "thinks he stands"
and "lest he fall," two words flash like a hazard light:
"take heed." The Greek word for that command comes
from the verb "to see." In other words, "Watch out!" This
study not only analyzes a mighty king's fall, it shouts an
urgent and timely warning to all who think they never
will. Rarely do people trip over things they have been
expecting. When we are on the lookout for some hazard,
we stay on our toes.

To begin with, we need to see that David's fall,
while severe, was certainly not sudden. Erosion had
weakened what once was strong. The great British
pastor and writer, F. B. Meyer, wisely said, "No man
suddenly becomes base." Just as no marriage suddenly
fractures, just as no tree suddenly rots, and just as no
church suddenly splits, no person suddenly falls.
There's a weakening. There's a crack in the foundation.
There's neglect.

At least three specific factors eroded David's strength as the mighty man of God.

Polygamy weakened David. It surprises people who are not students of this great man and have not studied the biblical text to hear that he had almost twenty wives, not to mention numerous concubines. The Torah specifically taught that a man, especially if he was king, was not to take more than one wife. David took many. Perhaps he thought, *After all, I live under this pressure and I work hard, and I have sacrificed much to get here. The least I can do is enjoy intimate pleasures with many women.* By then, who would confront the king and point out something in his private life?

Maybe that's why the text in 2 Samuel 5:13 states rather casually,

> Meanwhile David took more concubines and wives from Jerusalem, after he came from Hebron; . . .

Meanwhile?

Even though his wives and concubines increased, his passions were not abated. This king who took another man's wife already had a harem full of women. The simple fact is that the passion of sex is not satisfied by a full harem of women; it is increased. Having many women does not reduce a man's libido, it excites it . . . it stimulates it. David, being a man with a strong sexual appetite, mistakenly thought, *To satisfy it, I will have more women.* Thus, when he became the king, he added to the harem, but his drive only increased.

David was already given to lust. Polygamy weakened the otherwise mighty king.

Success weakened David. As we've seen, the man's reign became a model of sterling leadership for two decades. He gave choice men the oversight of finance, administration, and military defense. Through wise delegation, David multiplied his influence over Israel. With a beautiful home and family, a stable full of prize-winning horses, a military force everyone respected, and plans to build a temple for the Lord, who would dare point a finger of accusation at him? So what if he marries a few more women and quietly increases the number of his concubines? Isn't that the king's business? The economy's good and the future is bright . . . so leave him alone!

David's approval ratings soared to an all-time high—probably well over 95 percent. He had unrivaled power, an overflowing treasury, and an enormous following. And by this time, he had long since forgotten the hunger pangs, the scorching desert heat, and the long, cold nights sleeping in caves when Saul sought his life. Difficult times have a way of keeping a person humble and inspiring him or her to work hard. Pride and laziness have no place in a life lived close to the bone. But make no mistake: success and indulgence weakened David.

Idleness weakened David. Imagine the scene painted by the writer in just six words. "Then it happened in the spring." Outside David's window lay lush, green hills dappled with the dazzling colors of May. Springtime had awakened Jerusalem and adorned her with fresh color and the fragrance of flowers. Fields on their way to becoming another bumper crop surrounded the City of David while a gentle breeze, wafting into the king's bedroom, carried the hope of new life emerging from the soil. It was warm. It was lovely. Quiet. "Then it happened . . ." How eloquent.

Furthermore, "It was at the time when kings go out to battle." In those days, commanders-in-chief did not stay back with a body of bright military minds to conduct war electronically from a distance. Kings put on heavy armor, carried large shields, and led the troops into battle. The leader's place was at the front of the fight where he could be seen. Soldiers didn't have to wonder who was in command. Their king faced the enemy on the front line, bravely leading the charge. But not this time.

David had seen nothing but one battle after another for twenty years. He was a man of war. In full dress uniform, surely his medals covered his chest. But on this day, he was in his pajamas. Verse 1 tells us that David sent Joab and his servants to fight. David didn't worry about the battle. His general, Joab, a street-smart, cunning, and dispassionate warrior could handle it! While Joab led the battle, David was crawling out of bed. And it wasn't even morning. It was dusk. He'd been lying around all afternoon.

Something odd happens to people at dusk. During that between-time, temptations take advantage of the dim lighting to veil their consequences. Beware of minor indulgences at dusk. Tragedy lurks in the shadows.

David wasn't sleeping in that day because of exhaustion. He was indulging himself in idleness. Today we would say he sat down at his laptop and surfed the Net. And why not? Everything was under control. The nation virtually could run itself. Even the war was going well. Everywhere the king looked he saw a statue or a picture of himself.

Notice again the time of day in verse 2, "When evening came." Lounging around the bedroom in a nightshirt is not what David normally did in the evening. His songs tell us how he normally enjoyed the end of each day. Song Number 55 says,

> Evening and morning and at noon I will
> pray, and cry aloud, and He shall hear
> my voice. (Psalm 55:17 NKJV)

David normally prayed in the evening as he did in the morning and at noontime. In fact, he goes on in that psalm to say,

> He has redeemed my soul in peace from
> the battle that was against me.
> (Psalm 55:18)

Psalm 141 has similar lyrics:

> May my prayer be counted as incense
>   before You;
> The lifting up of my hands as the
>   evening offering.
> Set a guard, O Lord, over my mouth; . . .
> Do not incline my heart to any evil
>   thing. (Psalm 141:2–4)

In his paraphrase, Eugene Peterson renders verse 4 as, "Don't let me so much as dream of evil or thoughtlessly fall into bad company" (Psalm 141:4 MSG).

But David wasn't praying. Not on this particular evening. The mighty king forgot his own words in that psalm. The events of this dreadful evening would change David and his nation forever.

It isn't difficult to reconstruct the scene. David yawns, pushes back the bedspread, stretches himself full length as he rubs his eyes, runs his fingers through his auburn-colored hair, and slides around to sit on the edge of the bed. Blinks. Looks about the room.

He notices how the drapes are billowing in the evening breeze which invites him to casually get up, stroll lazily over to the open door, and step out into the warm evening air on his patio roof. It's silent up there. He's alone.

He hears splashing in the distance. The humming of soprano tones. His eyes turn in the direction his ears are leading him. Interestingly, he'd been too busy to even notice who lived behind him until this evening. He doesn't even know her name. Doesn't even know the family. *Now* he's interested.

Scripture says that she was a "woman who was *very* beautiful in appearance." Believe it. Remember that David had almost twenty wives and a harem of concubines in his palace, all of whom were among the most beautiful in Israel. This woman must have been stunning.

As David stared all alone in the dimness of dusk, he lost all cognizance of who he was or of what might happen should he yield. Focusing on the curves of her body, he forgot all the psalms he had written. He forgot all the lessons he had learned. He forgot all the respect he had earned. He forgot all the people who believed in him and even those who at this moment were praying for their king. He forgot his family. He forgot his own sons and daughters and the little children who played in the streets, seeing him as their hero — the matinee model of Israel — all that, he forgot. He forgot *God!*

Interesting, isn't it? When we wrestle with temptation, we invite God to kindly step out of the room. Dietrich Bonhoeffer, in a booklet titled simply, *Temptation*, describes this better than anyone.

In our members there is a slumbering
inclination toward desire, which is both
sudden and fierce. With irresistible
power desire seizes mastery over the
flesh. All at once a secret, smoldering
fire is kindled. The flesh burns and is in
flames . . .

At this moment God is quite unreal
to us . . . He loses all reality, and only
desire for the creature is real. The only
reality is the devil. Satan does not here
fill us with hatred of God, but with
forgetfulness of God . . .[2]

How true! David didn't *despise* God, he just conve-
niently *forgot* Him as he lost himself in this lingering,
lustful stare.

Before long, he asks, "Who . . . who is this woman?"
Some soft-footed servant comes to his side to answer.
The identification is more than curious. The servant
tactfully replies,

Is this not Bathsheba, the daughter of
Eliam, the *wife* of Uriah the Hittite?
(2 Samuel 11:3, emphasis added)

Hebrew genealogies very commonly identify people
by their father, almost never by their husband. It's a
fairly accurate assumption that his servant knew what
David was thinking. Perhaps not free enough to say,
"Don't go there," he simply adds more than he normally
would in identifying her by saying, "She's a married
woman. She has a husband."

David knew the ranks, and he didn't care that Uriah
was at battle. That circumstance made his intentions all
the more convenient.

Raymond Brown, who taught for a number of years at the Spurgeon College in London, adds a thought that has stirred some controversy.

> When we read this terrible story we instinctively think of the offence as David's sin, but this attractive woman cannot be entirely excused. Bathsheba was careless and foolish, lacking in the usual Hebrew modesty, or she certainly would not have washed in a place where she knew she could be overlooked. From her roof-top she would have looked out to see the royal palace and must have known that she could be seen. It is not enough merely to avoid sin ourselves. The New Testament insists that Christians must ensure that they do not become a stumbling block to others (Romans 14:12–13). If David had gone to war he would not have seen Bathsheba that night. If she had thought seriously about her actions she would not have put temptation in his path.[3]

Without a doubt, the greater responsibility rested with the Hebrew monarch. He was the aggressor. He did the pursuing. He opened the door by inviting her over. But it wasn't a rape, either. She didn't fight. She didn't try to talk him out of it or scream for help or flee the kingdom to preserve her purity.

The text runs swiftly through the narrative.

"David sent messengers and took her."

A knock at her door. She opens it, perhaps wrapped in a towel or her evening wear, looks into the face of the king's servant, and hears, "The king would like to see you."

The servant spirits her up the private back stairway in the new palace, she secretly slips into the room, and the door's closed and locked. A long embrace. Passionate kisses. Sex. But no love.

We're told that the woman purified herself from her uncleanness and returned to her house. David didn't give it a second thought. Lust works like that. But I wonder if, once inside her own dwelling, Bathsheba didn't lean hard against a wall, look up, and wonder, *What have I done?* And I wonder if, hours later in an unguarded moment, his own words invaded David's mind: *Ache naph-lu gi-boreem b'thoke hameel chamah.* How the mighty are fallen in battle.

But it's over. It's done. These things happen. Who will ever know? As another morning dawned, he wiped his hands of the matter, justified his adultery, and moved on.

But it wasn't over. Several weeks later, a knock came to his door along with a note. Bathsheba's three words would change everything: "I am pregnant."

That was David's moment, his opportunity, to prove himself again a man of God. He could stop the sin before it had a chance to multiply. He should have said what he would later say to Nathan when cornered, "I have sinned." Rather than gathering a group of wise and trusted counselors and laying his failure before them in full repentance, he panicked and attempted damage control.

David's mind was a whirlwind of fleshly motivated plans for a cover-up. Rather than choosing the right course, painful as it promised to be, he chose a path that would only complicate matters. David schemed to grant Bathsheba's husband a conjugal visit so the baby would appear to be his. But it backfired. Uriah, out of loyalty to his fellow soldiers, refused to enjoy anything they could not and chose instead to bunk with the king's servants. This must have infuriated David.

The king switched to plan B and plotted to have Uriah killed. He placed a note to Joab, his trusty general, in the hand of Uriah and sent him to rejoin the battle.

> Place Uriah in the front line of the
> fiercest battle and withdraw from him,
> so that he may be struck down and die.
> (2 Samuel 11:15)

Don't think that Joab didn't know what he was doing when he put the poor pawn on the front line at David's command. Shortly thereafter, when Joab sent news of the battle back to David, he added to the note, "Be sure to tell the king, 'Uriah was killed.'" Mission accomplished.

David feigned concern over the loss of victory as he breathed a giant sigh of relief. For effect he replied by way of the messenger, "Tell Joab to stay at it. Don't sweat this. These things happen, but he's doing a great job."

What a hypocrite! Still acting like a king though he's become a hollow shell of his former self. Thomas Baird once wrote, "Where the *barking* of the watchdog is not heeded, the *howl* of the bloodhound will soon be heard. When the warnings of Conscience are disregarded, then the accusations of Conscience must be endured."[4]

The bloodhound was howling! Uriah was out of the picture. Bathsheba would be showing soon. A hasty sham of a wedding ceremony attempted to veil a loveless marriage of convenience. Soon the newest queen began to stroll the palace in maternity clothes. Any adult can count to nine. What a phony.

Avoiding David's Downfall

Again, we might allow David's outrageous behavior to divert our attention from the task of examining ourselves. Seeing another person's weakness, poor decisions, and outright sin spelled out in bold, black print makes it too easy to write off their circumstances as somehow extraordinary. Chances are, you aren't a king, you don't have a harem, and you don't live in the lap of luxury. But the same human weaknesses that overtook David can do the same to you. The story of this mighty king's downfall has lots of lessons to teach, not the least of which is: *It can happen to the very, very best of us.* (Notice that's plural. That's you and me.)

When God chose David over Saul to rule as king, He called David a man after His own heart (see 1 Samuel 13:14, Acts 13:22). And throughout the rest of Israel's history, every king's righteousness was measured against David's. In terms of spirituality, David was the standard. Yet how the mighty had fallen.

If we say anything about the story of David's failure it shouldn't be, "My, look how ugly his sins are." We would be more correct, far wiser to say, "If it can happen to him, the danger must be even greater for me."

So how do we respond to this very real danger? The world will not grow less tempting, and we can't avoid the snares by retreating to the desert. Fortunately, sexual purity is something we can cultivate, beginning with these four strategies:

1. Acknowledge your weakness.

2. Guard your leisure.

3. Make yourself accountable to someone.

4. Rehearse the consequences often.

Acknowledge Your Weakness

We must avoid the assumption that we are ever morally safe. Any reasonable person might think, *because I'm a Christian, I'm strong*. Or, *because I'm married to a good partner, I'm strong*. Or, *because I have children, I'm strong*. Or, *because I have a responsible position, I'm strong. Because people respect me, I'm strong. Because I'm over fifty and have learned a lot of lessons, I'm strong!* The first part of those statements is true. But the last part of each one is not only false, it's foolhardy. No one—that includes *you*—is safe from failure!

At any given moment you or I can tumble into sin. Our sin nature is active and ready and willing.

Realize that at any given moment, day or night, you are at risk. It's far better to tell yourself that you're closer to a fall than you realize. It's far better—and certainly more true—to say, "Even though I'm a Christian, *I am weak*. I am a target of the enemy. Even though I am married, *I am weak*. I've known the joys of intimacy. I've experienced them; therefore, I know how fulfilling sex can be. Even though I have children, *I am weak*. Even though I have a position that many respect and that offers some measure of pleasure, *I am weak*. Even though I've known success, *I am weak*. Because I have failed before, *I am weak*."

Because we are weak, the Holy Spirit has been given to us in abundance. The pursuit of sexual purity begins by reminding ourselves of that every day. Yes . . . *every* day! Start by acknowledging, "I am weak."

Guard Your Leisure

Remember the old adage? "Idle hands are the devil's workshop." Time on your hands is downright perilous. Stay busy. Let me illustrate how dangerous idleness can be by telling you a true story.

Many years ago, when our children were small — all of them still school age — Cynthia stayed home with them while I flew to Canada for a full week of ministry. I was many miles from home and had just completed a busy week that began on Tuesday and ran through the evening hours of Friday. Breaking with my normal schedule, I extended my stay, agreeing to preach on Sunday, which left my Saturday free.

I was exhausted by Friday night. With the leisure of Saturday at my disposal, I decided to get a hamburger for lunch down at the hotel café and maybe look over the magazine rack and buy a sports newspaper or magazine.

I got my hamburger and headed for the rack, but all they had was hockey. (To say the least, I do not prefer hockey!) Frustrated that I couldn't find anything to read in a casual way, I turned toward the elevators and headed back to my room. I can still hear my heels snap across the marble of the big rotunda-like lobby leading to the hotel elevators. I pushed "up," stepped into the empty elevator and, before the doors closed, two very attractive women walked in. I pushed "6," stood back and asked, "What floor would you like?"

They said, almost in unison, "Six would be fine." Both smiled, looked at each other, then looked back at me with raised eyebrows, as if to be saying, "How 'bout it?" The elevator began to move up to the sixth floor.

Well, I have to confess that I suddenly felt a little like Mel Gibson or maybe Robert Redford; I won't lie to you. I stood there and I blinked, and for a moment the offer seemed inviting. That kind of thing doesn't happen to me very often, thank God. But something else far more powerful happened within me. I pulled down the shade of my mind, and I read the words my mother had drilled into me as a little boy when she and I memorized Scripture together over the kitchen table. Those words were, "Do not be deceived, God is not mocked; for whatever a man sows, that he will also reap" (Galatians 6:7 NKJV). Whoop! Shade went up.

I know the women must have wondered what I was reading as I stood there. And one of them said, "Well . . . how 'bout it?"

I said, "No thanks, I'm really not interested in you ladies. I've got more than I can keep up with at home."

They stared at me like I was from Mars. The doors abruptly opened and I stepped out . . . alone. Even though they asked for the sixth floor, the women stayed on the elevator as the doors slowly closed. As soon as those doors shut, I leaned against the wall in a cold sweat thinking, *Thanks Mom. Thank You, Lord, for Your powerful Word!*

I shudder when I think about what could have happened. I could never have written this chapter. I could never have served as chancellor of Dallas Theological Seminary, formed Stonebriar Community Church, or even preached another sermon. I could have lost the respect of my children and equally important, the trust of my wife, Cynthia. Had I made the wrong decision, my entire future of ministry would have been altered. Frightening thoughts.

Work hard. Stay busy. Guard your leisure. If you find yourself with hours of time on your hands, get involved in something bigger than yourself, apply your energy to something important. Slip on your sneakers and go for a run. Don't allow evil an opportunity to embezzle your purity.

Now, no one can stay busy all the time. Everyone needs leisure — time to relax the body, rest the mind, and do nothing productive. I'm not suggesting that leisure is evil. But if sin has an opportunity to lure you, it's most effective when you are idle. Take time to recharge your batteries. Enjoy your leisure . . . but guard it like a hawk.

A Special Word about the Internet

I can think of no greater danger to an idle mind than the Internet. This marvelous technology has brought immeasurable potential for learning to our fingertips. But for all its potential to enrich our minds, it has the power to corrupt them.

The statistics of those who are addicted is staggering, not to mention those who turn to it in the secrecy of their undetected world. Knowing how pervasive and insidious this temptation really is requires me to stay alert and ready. Every month 2,500 more pornographic sites enter the Internet. And many of them are tucked away, ready to fill your screen even when you're not seeking it.

While trying to find a map to a little town in north Texas where several friends and I could ride our Harleys and then eat a barbeque lunch together, I punched in the name of that town. That's it—that's all I entered into my desktop computer. Immediately, in bold, one-inch letters, I saw "SEX" on my screen. And that was only the beginning. As I tried to remove it, each new attempt brought up more lurid scenes. Even when I pressed the "ESCAPE" key I was unable to escape the recurring scenes, each one intensely alluring to the flesh.

Determined, I reached down and turned my computer off . . . completely off. Finally! But, would you believe it? When I later turned it on, there it was again—another unwanted but very real temptation. Thankfully, my younger son, Chuck, Jr., was able to find a way to free the equipment. And it all started while on a simple, rather hurried search for a little town in north Texas. The danger is ever-present and more insidious with each passing day.

But don't make the mistake of thinking that only pictures and movies constitute pornography or that it's only for men. More and more women are yielding to the lure of virtual sex by way of chat rooms and instant messenger programs. Given the right set of emotional conditions, innocent exchanges with an anonymous man via e-mail can evolve into much more. An emotional affair, fed by false intimacy, incubated in the secrecy and anonymity of cyberspace, can stifle a pure mind just as quickly as lurid images.

Make Yourself Accountable to Someone

Can you name two or three same-gender individuals with whom you meet regularly to talk about things that no one else will talk about with you? If you can, then you are accountable. If you can't, you are at risk.

In his book, *Love Must Be Tough*, my good friend Dr. James Dobson outlines what he calls the anatomy of adultery based on his many years of counseling experience. When describing the first step that a woman takes down that awful pathway, he invariably finds that "she is lonely, suffers from low self-esteem, and has had difficulty making female friends."[5] She has no accountability, no appropriate outlet for her deepest, most troubling feelings. And without accountability, she's a tragedy waiting for an attentive womanizer.

Now, accountability doesn't mean you have to subject yourself to an inquisition by your friends. It should not become a meeting of the holier-than-thou club. Meet regularly, talk openly, do things together, and have fun, but develop trust so you can be completely honest. And when you meet, dare to ask each other hard questions. Here are a few. These are worded for men, but they work equally well for women.

- Have you been with a woman anywhere this past week that might be seen as compromising?

- Have you exposed yourself to any sexually explicit material?

- Have you had conversations or correspondence with anyone that would make your spouse feel threatened?

- Have you spent adequate time in the study of the Scriptures and in prayer?

- Have you given priority to your family?

- Have you fulfilled the mandates of your vocation?

- Have you just lied to me?

Develop same-gender friendships that allow you to be completely candid as you ask and answer questions like these. If you do that regularly, you're safer. I didn't say you were perfectly protected from a fall; I said you're safer. I've known some who have been accountable who have fallen. It was only an act . . . a phony accountability. They went through the motions, but they lied. But if you speak truth, hear truth, and deal with truth, you're safer.

Make yourself accountable to someone.

Rehearse the Consequences Beforehand

The fellow minister I mentioned earlier didn't rehearse the consequences. The once-mighty king, David, didn't rehearse the consequences. Had I yielded at that moment on the hotel elevator in Canada, it would have been because I didn't rehearse the consequences. Consequences hold our feet to the fire. They boldly confront what we'd rather ignore. They don't lie. They represent the reality that lust doesn't want to hear.

A number of years ago, Randy Alcorn wrote a little sidebar called "Consequences of a Moral Tumble" in a magazine titled *Leadership*. I've carried it with me since 1988. He writes,

> Whenever I feel particularly vulnerable to sexual temptation, I find it helpful to review what effects my actions could have:
>
> • Grieving the Lord who redeemed me.
>
> • Dragging His sacred name into the mud.
>
> • One day having to look Jesus, the Righteous Judge, in the face and give an account of my actions.

- Following in the footsteps of these people whose immorality forfeited their ministries and caused me to shudder: (list names).

- Inflicting untold hurt on Nanci, my best friend, and loyal wife.

- Losing Nanci's respect and trust.

- Hurting my beloved daughters Karina and Angie.

- Destroying my example and credibility with my children, and nullifying both present and future efforts to teach them to obey God ("Why listen to a man who betrayed Mom and us?")

- If my blindness should continue or my wife be unable to forgive, perhaps losing my wife and my children forever.

- Causing shame to my family ("Why isn't Daddy a pastor anymore?")

- Losing self-respect.

- Creating a form of guilt awfully hard to shake. Even though God would forgive me, would I forgive myself?

- Forming memories and flashbacks that could plague future intimacy with my wife.

- Wasting years of ministry training and experience for a long time, maybe permanently.

- Forfeiting the effect of years of witnessing to my father and reinforcing his distrust for ministers that has only begun to soften by my example but that would harden, perhaps permanently, because of my immorality.

- Undermining the faithful example and hard work of other Christians in our community.

- Bringing great pleasure to Satan, the enemy of God and all that is good.

- Possibly bearing the physical consequences of such diseases as gonorrhea, syphilis, chlamydia, herpes, and AIDS; perhaps infecting Nanci or, in the case of AIDS, even causing her death.

- Possibly causing pregnancy, with the personal and financial implications, including a lifelong reminder of my sin.

- Bringing shame and hurt to these fellow pastors and elders: (list names).

- Causing shame and hurt to these friends, especially those I've led to Christ and discipled: (list names)

- Invoking shame and life-long embarrassment upon myself.[6]

Trust me, if you review such consequences regularly, your lust will take a backseat . . . but it still won't go away.

The shrill ring of the telephone broke the silence in my study. But it was the message that broke my heart. My earnest prayer is that no one will ever make a phone call like that about you or about me. I urge you to complete the Bible study in the section that follows this chapter, then read on to discover how to gain the victory over temptation as we examine the life of Joseph.

My Questions and Thoughts

My Questions and Thoughts

Chapter 2

Take Heed

You Are Here

Chuck Colson tells of an old friend—who seemed to be a mature Christian—who left his wife of many years for another woman. The shock sparked Colson to question how a man so devoted to his wife and to the Lord could turn to adultery. Referring to an essay by the late Sheldon Vanauken, Colson noted:

> Vanauken describes how a Christian friend named John shocked him by announcing that he was leaving his wife to marry another woman. John explained his sudden change of heart by saying, "It seemed so good, so right. That's when we knew we had to get the divorces. We belonged together."

> Vanauken then describes a conversation with a friend named Diana, who left her husband for another man. Diana defended herself with virtually the same words: "It was just so good and right with Roger that I knew it would be wrong to go on with Paul."

As Vanauken explains, both John and Diana were "invoking a higher law: the feeling of goodness and rightness. A feeling so powerful that it swept away... whatever guilt they would otherwise have felt" for what they were doing to their families.[1]

Statistics reveal that affairs are not rare occurrences. Dr. Shirley Glass wrote, "After reviewing twenty-five studies . . . I concluded that 25 percent of wives and 44 percent of husbands have had extramarital intercourse. This is startling news indeed."[2] And living in such a culture, Christians are not exempt from its influences—or from contributing to its carnality.

When we turn to Scripture, many read the account of David and Bathsheba with the same interest that keeps them in their seats during a naughty movie. But the Bible doesn't include David's immorality like some gratuitous scene in a Hollywood film, giving us permission to gape when we normally should walk out. We are *meant* to recoil at this account—not indulge. The very fact the scene piques our interest ought to make us aware of our own need for its lessons.

Give your response to this statement:
"What happened to David could happen to me."

☐ Absolutely

☐ No way

☐ Honestly, I'm not sure

How do the moral failures or successes in your life or in the lives of others contribute to your answer?

How does your knowledge of the Bible or theology contribute to your answer?

Discovering the Way

In our autopsy of a moral fall in the previous chapter, we briefly visited the apostle Paul's words in 1 Corinthians 10:12: "Therefore let him who thinks he stands take heed that he does not fall." Paul led up to this key verse by offering the Corinthians a lesson from the history of a young Jewish nation.

Read 1 Corinthians 10:1–4:

> For I do not want you to be unaware,
> brethren, that our fathers were all under
> the cloud and all passed through the
> sea; and all were baptized into Moses
> in the cloud and in the sea; and all ate
> the same spiritual food; and all drank
> the same spiritual drink, for they were
> drinking from a spiritual rock which
> followed them; and the rock was Christ.

Paul's original word for "be unaware" is *agnoeō*, from which we get the word *ignorant*. Sometimes we simply lack information. So Paul pointed the Corinthians back to the example of the Hebrew fathers during the Exodus. He said they *all* had shared experiences.

Take a pen and circle each occurrence of the word *all* in verses 1–4 listed above.

What five privileges do these verses indicate *all* the Hebrews shared?

1.

2.

3.

4.

5.

Place a check mark next to the practices in which you have participated (or in which you regularly participate) as a Christian:

☐ Baptism   ☐ Faith in Christ

☐ Communion   ☐ Bible study

☐ Moral lifestyle   ☐ Fellowship

☐ Church attendance   ☐ Prayer

More than likely you checked most if not all of these activities. If so, you enjoy a privileged position unlike many others across the world. What an advantage you have by attending a good Bible-teaching church! What a privilege you have by receiving solid instruction in the Word to grow in your walk with Christ!

When Israel traveled in the wilderness, the same God who redeemed them by His grace provided abundantly for their needs. And the same remains true for us. However, Paul indicated a strange turn of events in the next verse.

Read 1 Corinthians 10:5:

> Nevertheless, with most of them God
> was not well-pleased; for they were laid
> low in the wilderness.

Despite the fact that *all* the Hebrews participated in God's gracious deliverance and provision, it seems incredible that *most of them* ended up as bleached bones in the desert. Why? The text provides a timeless truth we would do well to mull over:

*Position and privileges provide no guarantee
against the possibility of sin.*

Like the Jews and King David, we enjoy great
privileges from the Lord—both in salvation and in
provision.

**Look up the following verses from Ephesians 1. What
blessings did we receive as believers?**

Ephesians 1:3

Ephesians 1:7

Ephesians 1:13–14

We often associate spiritual maturity with spiritual
strength—and strength with safety. But we ought to
wake up to the dangers for the mature.

———————————— ∞ ————————————

*While our sins do not threaten the security of our
salvation, we must remember our salvation does not
protect us from the possibility of sinning. Even forgiven
sin can have lasting consequences.*

———————————— ∞ ————————————

Paul then listed some specific sins the Hebrews committed. They serve as sobering examples for believers to avoid.

Read 1 Corinthians 10:6–11:

> Now these things happened as examples for us, so that we would not crave evil things as they also craved. Do not be idolaters, as some of them were; as it is written, "THE PEOPLE SAT DOWN TO EAT AND STOOD UP TO PLAY." Nor let us act immorally, as some of them did, and twenty-three thousand fell in one day. Nor let us try the Lord, as some of them did, and were destroyed by the serpents. Nor grumble, as some of them did, and were destroyed by the destroyer. Now these things happened to them as an example, and they were written for our instruction, upon whom the ends of the ages have come.

Circle each occurrence of the phrases "as they also" or "as some of them" in verses 6–11.

Now list the sinful activities in which the Hebrews participated in verses 6–10:

1.

2.

3.

4.

In his book *Finishing Strong*, Steve Farrar relates the results of a study Dr. Howard Hendricks conducted of 246 men in full-time ministry who had become involved in sexual immorality within a two-year period. Keep in mind that each man was committed to Christ.

> After interviewing each man, Dr. Hendricks discovered four correlations running through the experiences of the entire 246 who derailed:
>
> 1. None were involved in any kind of personal accountability group.
>
> 2. Each had ceased to invest in a daily personal time of prayer, Scripture reading, and worship.
>
> 3. Over 80 percent of them became sexually involved with another woman as the result of counseling the woman. In other words, they were spending significant portions of their schedules with women other than their wives.

4. Without exception, each of the 246
   had been convinced that moral
   failure "will never happen to me." [3]

Let's read that last line again — slowly . . .

Moral failure "will never happen to me."

A researcher at the University of Denver commented that many people who report being in happy marriages commit adultery. She noted, "Those who assume that only bad people in bad marriages cheat can blind themselves to their own risk. . . . They're unprepared for the risky times in their own lives." [4] The relationship between "happy marriages" and affairs finds its link in the words: *blind to their own risk . . . unprepared.*

This study not only analyzes a mighty king's fall, it shouts an urgent and timely warning to all who think they never will. Rarely do people trip over things they have been expecting.

— Chuck Swindoll

When we hear through the grapevine or on the news of a Christian who has fallen, the thought quickly comes to our minds (and mouths), "You're kidding! (*Deep sigh*) I can't believe it; I would *never* do that." We console ourselves with the fact that we never *want* to do that. "After all, God will protect me — He always has. And I try to live as a good person; my sins aren't *that* bad."

Doorway to History

In the time of David, Jerusalem was only a fraction of the city's size today. In fact, many find it surprising that the entire city encompassed only ten acres outside the current walls of Jerusalem, just south of the Temple Mount. This "City of David" sat along a hill with steep slopes—an ideal location for defense throughout the centuries. Archeological discoveries at the crest of the hill uncovered a large, stepped-stone structure dating to the time of King David (1000 B.C.). The structure likely supported a royal building, and as such, it probably held the residence of David. The hilltop site reveals how David could easily see the rest of the city beneath him—including Bathsheba on her roof. David's location gave him a vantage point no one else had; and with that privilege came a temptation to which David succumbed.

Much of the temptation regarding sexual impurity finds its roots in privileges we can take advantage of. A private office, a business trip, a personal secretary, a therapist, a view into a neighbor's house or backyard—and numerous other situations—all offer repeated opportunities for personal gratification at the expense of someone else. We ought to ask ourselves some questions. What privileges has God provided that we have abused? What can we do to remain above reproach and to use these positions for God's advantage rather than our own?

Scripture portrays David's plunge for a reason: *It stands as a warning to all who would come after him.* That's all of us. If it could happen to David—a man after God's own heart (1 Samuel 13:14)—it could happen to us.

Consider how many lives and deaths go unrecorded. Why did God inspire these lives to appear in the Bible—and then inspire Paul to remind us of them? Twice Paul said that these things were written for our instruction (1 Corinthians 10:6, 11). The original word for *instruction* can also refer to a *warning*. As Paul drove home his point to the Corinthians, so the text warns us of our own potential for stumbling.

Read 1 Corinthians 10:12:

> Therefore let him who thinks he stands
> take heed that he does not fall.

Getting to the Root

The Greek word for "thinks" in 1 Corinthians 10:12 is *dokeō*. One who thinks in this way exercises an opinion—not necessarily a fact.[5] The Greek word translated "take heed" might be paraphrased, "Open your eyes!" We cannot remain blind to our own risk.

An honest person recognizes that confidence provides no shelter from sin but leaves us vulnerable to it. What happened to David could happen to any believer—regardless of beliefs, education, or past spiritual victory.

Even the apostle Paul acknowledged his own potential for stumbling. Just prior to our passage in 1 Corinthians 10, Paul ended chapter 9 with these words:

> I discipline my body and make it my slave, so that, after I have preached to others, I myself will not be disqualified. (1 Corinthians 9:27)

The verb Paul used for "discipline" described an incredibly demanding effort. Paul described the physical struggle with a word that pictured the blows of a boxer. Consider a few other renderings:

> I beat my body . . . (NIV)

> I chastise my body . . . (YOUNG'S LT)

> I treat my body hard . . . (NCV)

> I harden my body with blows . . . (GNT)

Starting Your Journey

Paul's striving for the *discipline* of his physical body was not a walk in the park. He compared it to a brawl, with the result that his body would serve him—not vice versa. Any defeat would come with a terrible price. Paul wrote: "So that, after I have preached to others, I myself will not be disqualified" (1 Corinthians 9:27). Paul's concern over sin came primarily from the possibility of the loss of his witness. His physical body would represent either a platform or a barrier for people to hear of Jesus Christ.

Write two examples of people you know whose lives cratered morally:

1.

2.

Write two examples of those you know whose lives you deeply admire:

1.

2.

What do you think made the difference?

We began in 1 Corinthians 10:1 by looking at Paul's use of the word *unaware*. The prevention of a fall begins with the awareness of its possibility. Interestingly, in addition to having the meaning "ignorant," the original word, *agnoeō*, also provides us the word *ignore* (a meaning Paul used a few chapters later in 14:38). Sometimes we unwillingly lack information, but more often, we willingly ignore the truth clearly set before us.

Having performed an autopsy on David's fall, let's turn the scalpel on our own hearts. Let's examine our current situation. How can *we* "take heed"?

Answer the following questions yes or no, and be *brutally honest* with yourself. Write out your answer.

Are you willing to acknowledge your weakness to sexual temptation?

Do you consciously guard your leisure time and activities from opportunities that could lead to sin?

Do you make yourself accountable to someone who can spot a lie and who will call you out on it?

Do you regularly rehearse the consequences of moral failure?

Straight yes answers do not mean you are safe from a moral collapse, but if you answered no to any of these questions, you will be even more susceptible to a moral failure. You need to seriously address any no answers . . . or any of the yes answers on which you even hesitated.

Answer the last three questions again by inserting the words *when* and *how* at the beginning of each.

When do you consciously guard your leisure time and activities from opportunities that could lead to sin?

How?

When do you make yourself accountable to someone who can spot a lie and who will call you out on it?

How?

When do you regularly rehearse the consequences of moral failure?

How?

Of course, taking heed means more than answering questions. It means you can point to your calendar and show an accountability meeting. It means you have a plan for staying faithful on that upcoming business trip. Taking heed means you see others' failures as a warning of your own potential. Taking heed means you know you can fall like the Hebrews did, like David did, and like so many others around us do.

Read the following excerpt from Charles Spurgeon, highlighting any lines that particularly stand out to you:

> "Keep back Thy servant also from presumptuous sins" (Psalm 19:13). Such was the prayer of the "man after God's own heart." Did holy David need to pray thus? How needful, then, must such a prayer be for *us* babes in grace! It is as if he said, "Keep me back, or I shall rush headlong over the precipice of sin." Our evil nature, like an ill-tempered horse, is apt to run away. May the grace of

God put the bridle upon it, and hold it in, that it rush not into mischief. What might not the best of us do if it were not for the checks which the Lord sets upon us both in providence and in grace! The psalmist's prayer is directed against the worst form of sin—that which is done with deliberation and willfulness. Even the holiest need to be "kept back" from the vilest transgressions. It is a solemn thing to find the apostle Paul warning saints against the most loathsome sins. "Mortify therefore your members which are upon the earth; fornication, uncleanness, inordinate affection, evil concupiscence, and covetousness, which is idolatry." What! Do saints want warning against such sins as these? Yes, they do. The whitest robes, unless their purity be preserved by divine grace, will be defiled by the blackest spots. Experienced Christian, boast not in your experience; you will trip yet if you look away from Him who is able to keep you from falling. Ye whose love is fervent, whose faith is constant, whose hopes are bright, say not, "We shall never sin," but rather cry, "Lead us not into temptation." There is enough tinder in the heart of the best of men to light a fire that shall burn to the lowest hell, unless God shall quench the sparks as they fall. Who would have dreamed

that righteous Lot could be found
drunken, and committing uncleanness?
Hazael said, "Is Thy servant a dog, that
he should do this thing?" and we are
very apt to use the same self-righteous
question. May infinite wisdom cure us
of the madness of self-confidence.[6]

Review your marks of Spurgeon's words. What was it from these sections that addressed you personally?

Give your response to this statement:
"What happened to David could happen to me."

☐ Absolutely

☐ No way

☐ Honestly, I'm not sure

Therefore let him who thinks he
stands take heed that he does not fall.
(1 Corinthians 10:12)

We've taken a good, hard look at our own very real
potential for moral failure and exposed the universal
weakness of humanity. Now let's turn our attention
from the possibility of sexual impurity to its prevention,
examining a critical point in the life of another man of
God—Joseph.

My Questions and Thoughts

My Questions and Thoughts

_____

_____

_____

_____

_____

_____

_____

_____

_____

_____

_____

_____

_____

_____

_____

_____

_____

_____

_____

_____

_____

_____

_____

_____

Chapter 3

Don't Resist Temptation . . . Run!

In the first chapter, I briefly touched on Dietrich Bonhoeffer's excellent description of temptation. His depiction deserves more attention.

> In our members there is a slumbering inclination toward desire which is both sudden and fierce. With irresistible power desire seizes mastery over the flesh. All at once a secret, smoldering fire is kindled. The flesh burns and is in flames. It makes no difference whether it is sexual desire, or ambition, or vanity, or desire for revenge, or love of fame and power, or greed for money, or, finally, that strange desire for the beauty of the world, of nature. Joy in God is in the course of being extinguished in us and we seek all our joy in the creature. At this moment God is quite unreal to us. He loses all reality, and only desire for the creature is real. The only reality is the devil. Satan does not here fill us with hatred of God, but with forgetfulness of God. And now his falsehood is

added to this proof of strength. The lust
thus aroused envelops the mind and
will of man in deepest darkness. The
powers of clear discrimination and of
decision are taken from us. . . .
It is here that everything within me
rises up against the Word of God.[1]

Everyone who has lived long enough to have a
rational thought has suffered the mesmerizing pull of
temptation. Temptation is an inevitable consequence of
living in a world enveloped by evil, and everyone, except
Jesus Christ, has yielded to sin's enticing promises
at one time or another. The charm of temptation and
its promises are as unique as the people it hopes
to ensnare.

Material temptation, the lust for things, may be as
big as a house or as small as a ring. A dazzling new car;
a quaint, old antique; the latest time-saver; a high-tech
gadget; or a room full of new furniture. Who hasn't felt
just a little entitled to spend more than is wise? After
all, you've worked hard. Who's going to thank you if
you don't?

Power hunger is the temptation to usurp authority or quietly take control through manipulation. It
can also result in desiring a notable title or position,
such as "chief executive" or "president" or "doctor" or
"professor." Nothing wrong with titles or positions, until
temptation whispers in your ear, "Imagine the respect
and admiration this will bring you. Then everyone will
know what you know: you're very special."

But in this chapter, we're concerned with the more
familiar type of temptation. Genesis 39, like 2 Samuel 5,
tells the story of a successful and godly man faced with
the intoxicating appeal of physical sensuality. He was

tempted to fulfill God-given sexual desires outside the God-ordained context of marriage.

A Lesson on Purity from the Life of Joseph

Before we examine this episode in the life of Joseph, I believe it's important to understand how it fits into the big picture. Everything an author chooses to include in a story must either reveal something about one of the characters or develop the plot. And good authors, like Moses, will often show the character in action to reveal his or her nature. The story of Joseph spans thirteen chapters in the book of Genesis, from chapter 37 through the end of the book. Chapter 38 forms a break in his story to focus on the life of his brother, Judah. In this chapter, Judah married a Canaanite woman and had three sons by her. The first was so immoral, God took his life. The second abused a sacred tradition to satisfy his sexual desire, so the Lord removed him too. Judah later slept with a woman he thought was a harlot for the price of a goat, only to discover later that she was his daughter-in-law in disguise—who was pregnant with his child. Talk about a dysfunctional family! Whoever said the Bible is dull and irrelevant never read Genesis.

Moses then returns to the life of Joseph, where he introduces this story of sexual temptation. I believe he does this to show us, by contrast, the purity of his character. In fact, this episode doesn't merely tell us how Joseph handled one temptation. The inspired author describes this incident to show us how Joseph consistently responded to sexual enticement. Perhaps this episode was a first that defined the rest and put him on a collision course—a God-ordained collision course—with his destiny.

Joseph's Circumstances

The first six verses of Genesis 39 establish the historic situation. In the first verse, I notice two details conspicuously absent.

> Now Joseph had been taken down
> to Egypt; and Potiphar, an Egyptian
> officer of Pharaoh, the captain of the
> bodyguard, bought him from the
> Ishmaelites, who had taken him down
> there. (Genesis 39:1)

First, I see no mention of the time that transpired between chapters 37 and 39. After coming to Egypt, Joseph could have been in Potiphar's home for a matter of weeks, months, or even years before temptation came his way.

Second, Moses gives us no details about the obvious adjustments that Joseph had to make. Remember, he came from a rural home and the protection of a doting, older father. Jacob had indulged the boy with special favors, provided him with special clothing, and kept him from the hardest work. From this insulated, safe environment, Joseph was dumped into a pit, sold to a caravan on its way to Egypt, and finally purchased from the slave block like a common piece of merchandise.

Imagine the adjustments! A new language, a new culture, new relationships, new surroundings, and new responsibilities. And talk about pressure! He was owned by a man described as the "captain of the bodyguard." A literal Hebrew translation could be "chief slaughterer." Admittedly, that could mean Potiphar was the head cook, but it's far more likely he was the chief of security. He led an elite, disciplined military unit of crack troops to guard the Pharaoh. He was responsible for carrying out justice — including overseeing Egypt's prisons and executing criminals and political enemies. In other words, he was no mere government official. This was not a man to cross.

Obviously, Joseph handled the adjustments well.

> The Lord was with Joseph, so he
> became a successful man. And he was
> in the house of his master, the Egyptian.
> Now his master saw that the Lord was
> with him and how the Lord caused
> all that he did to prosper in his hand.
> (Genesis 39:2–3)

We could summarize the verses this way:

> The Lord prospered Joseph's work
>
> +   Joseph worked in Potiphar's house
> _____
> =   Potiphar put 2 and 2 together

Notice that Joseph didn't have to say anything. He simply did his work *and* let God prosper it and receive the credit. No presumption. No grandstanding or finagling. He didn't use his spirituality as a tool. Instead, the Lord revealed to Potiphar that He was with Joseph. As a result, this tough, idol-worshiping slave-owner gained a respect for God and soon rewarded His servant, Joseph.

> So Joseph found favor in his sight and
> became his personal servant; and he
> made him overseer over his house, and
> all that he owned he put in his charge.
> (Genesis 39:4)

Quite a promotion! Joseph found himself on a fast track to the top of the organization. Personal valet to the chief of security in one of the world's most advanced civilizations. And look. It gets better:

> It came about that from the time he
> made him overseer in his house and
> over all that he owned, the Lord blessed
> the Egyptian's house on account of
> Joseph; thus the Lord's blessing was
> upon all that he owned, in the house
> and in the field.
>
> So he left everything he owned in
> Joseph's charge; and with him there he
> did not concern himself with anything
> except the food which he ate.
>
> Now Joseph was handsome in form
> and appearance. (Genesis 39:5–6)

Notice two general principles of life at work here. First, with greater success comes greater trust. Second, with greater trust comes less accountability . . . which invariably results in increased vulnerability.

Count on it. Success is dangerous.

F. B. Meyer writes,

> We may expect temptation in the days
> of prosperity and ease rather than in
> those of privation and toil. . . . Not
> where men frown, but where they smile
> sweet exquisite smiles of flattery—it is
> *there*, it is *there*, that the temptress lies
> in wait! Beware! If thou goest armed
> anywhere, thou must, above all, go
> armed here.[2]

Remember David? Remember his rise to success? What a wise warning. This message does not go out to the bum in the gutter. This warning goes out to the successful, to the up-and-coming executive, to the young and very gifted minister in the growing church, to the individual who is receiving the benefits of God, who has been given greater privilege and enjoys increased privacy. Carlyle, the Scottish essayist, was right, "Adversity is sometimes hard upon a man; but for one man who can stand prosperity, there are a hundred that will stand adversity."[3]

Joseph's Challenge

Clearly, Joseph was a prime target for temptation. He was a slave who had earned the right to be respected and eventually required little if any monitoring. Potiphar turned everything regarding his house and finances over to Joseph. Apparently, Joseph determined his own schedule, organized and oversaw the daily operation of both the home and the fields, running the entire estate and keeping the books as though everything were his own.

Stop! Pause here and observe how verse 6 closes. I love how the inspired author of Genesis leaves barely a breath between this elaborate description of Joseph's success and the danger he faced. In effect, Moses says, "Oh, did I happen to mention that he was extremely handsome?" If this were a movie, the music would suddenly turn dark and foreboding.

> It came about after these events that
> his master's wife looked with desire at
> Joseph, and she said, "Lie with me." But
> he refused and said to his master's wife,
> "Behold, with me here, my master does
> not concern himself with anything in
> the house, and he has put all that he
> owns in my charge. (Genesis 39:7–8)

"Have sex with me." That's direct enough! But I love the very next words: "But he refused." Simple proposition. Simple response.

We might be tempted to put Joseph on a spiritual pedestal and suppose that somehow God protected him with a supernatural, moral force-field. As Clarence Macartney put it, "Joseph was not a stone, a mummy, but a red-blooded young man in his late twenties."[4] Yes, God prospered his work and gave him astounding success. But He did the same for David. Certainly God gave Joseph every advantage to choose wisely. But He did the same for David. And He does the same for us.

In the previous chapter, we studied Paul's warning to the Corinthian church. He concluded his lesson by saying,

> No temptation has overtaken you but such as is common to man; and God is faithful, who will not allow you to be tempted beyond what you are able, but with the temptation will provide the way of escape also, so that you will be able to endure it. (1 Corinthians 10:13)

That has always been God's promise. That was true for Joseph, and we can claim it and act on it just as he did. He refused! He said NO! Joseph wasted no time shutting down her advances!

Notice how clear Joseph was about his motives and the consequences of failure.

> But he refused and said to his master's wife, "Behold, with me here, my master does not concern himself with anything in the house, and he has put all that he owns in my charge. There is no one

greater in this house than I, and he has
withheld nothing from me except you,
because you are his wife. How then
could I do this great evil and sin against
God?" (Genesis 39:8–9)

Not far from Joseph's mind was loyalty to his boss.
Potiphar had been good to him. How could he repay
the kindness of his master by defiling the man's wife?
Trust is a precious commodity, and it fueled Joseph's
privileged way of life. And let's not forget his master's
occupation! If there is anyone's trust you would not
want to violate, it's the chief slaughterer's!

We also have to remember his primary motiva-
tion. Joseph says, "How could I do this great evil and
sin against God?" Clarence Macartney describes the
encounter while applying a little imagination. Admittedly, this is only conjecture, but I think it helps us
appreciate the humanity of the scene:

> An old story tells how when Joseph
> began to talk about God to the temptress,
> she flung her skirt over the bust of the
> god that stood in the chamber and said,
> "Now, God will not see!" But Joseph
> answered, "My God always sees!" [5]

How could he resist? His God saw him. He didn't
entertain the temptation, so his God remained real to
him. Even in the privacy of a bedchamber, with the
master's wife seductively offering him the pleasure of her
body, he didn't forget God. He was unmarried, virile,
handsome, unaccountable to his family, and unseen by
the woman's husband. The most natural thing in the
world was to yield. Instead, he called it what it was.
"This is an evil, a sin against God."

I see a principle here. Perhaps it's not enough merely to avoid looking toward temptation, but to keep our minds so focused on God-honoring goals that we're not distracted by anything less. Joseph valued his professional integrity and fought to protect it. Furthermore, he loved his God and wanted to please Him.

"Okay," you say. "Glad that's over! Thank God for Joseph's example. Deal with temptation like you should and move on." If only temptation were so easily discouraged. As the next verse reveals, the seductive woman kept it up.

> As she spoke to Joseph day after day, he
> did not listen to her to lie beside her or
> be with her. (Genesis 39:10)

Temptation never surrenders so quickly. If anything, you will become more of a challenge to the tempter. In this case, the fact that Joseph wasn't a weak-willed wimp probably fueled the desire of the temptress even more. The tempter or temptress yearns for the respected person, the person who is quoted by others, the successful, capable person. The conquest likely feeds his or her hollow self-image. So we shouldn't be surprised that she persisted. He was a catch!

Looking at temptation from her perspective reminds me of another principle that will be useful to our understanding. It's found in James 1:13–14:

> Let no one say when he is tempted, "I
> am being tempted by God"; for God
> cannot be tempted by evil, and He
> Himself does not tempt anyone. But
> each one is tempted when he is car-
> ried away and enticed by *his own lust*.
> (emphasis added)

The pull of temptation is really a force between two objects—an inner desire and an outer bait. Understand, there's no sin in the bait. The sin is in the bite. Certainly one method of avoiding sin is to stay away from the bait. But, let's face it, you can't always avoid sensual enticement if you live in the real world. In the case of Potiphar's wife, Joseph's good looks were not the problem. Her inner desire—unchecked by devotion to God and probably nurtured by indulgence—demanded satisfaction despite the consequences.

We will discuss several ways to deal with temptation when faced with it, but I will only speak at the level of biblical principle. Cultivating a lifestyle of moral purity, according to Scripture, requires that the Holy Spirit transform our hearts so that we love God and hate the things He hates. But we cannot ignore the pathology of sin. Some choices to sin may have gone beyond the level of habit, and perhaps a particular sin now rules you as a compulsion you cannot resist without intervention. You need someone to help you out of the cycle. Competent, Christian professionals can help individuals uncover destructive motivations and replace them with God-honoring ones.

At the end of this book, you will find contact information for our Pastoral Ministries Department at Insight for Living. Each of these seminary-trained pastors and women's counselors count it a privilege to respond to your letters and receive your phone calls on any matter that troubles you. You don't have to face this struggle alone. In fact, it's foolish to try.

Joseph's Response

In Genesis 39:10–13, I find Joseph's key strategy against temptation. He recognized his weakness, he respected the power of his enemy, and he acted accordingly. Joseph knew better than to pick fights with giants.

Four little words at the end of verse 10 are easily overlooked. They form a first line of defense against both temptation and becoming fodder for gossip: "or be with her." This could be either a euphemism for sexual intercourse, like "lie beside her," or it can be taken in the literal sense that he refused even to be alone with her. Scholars split on the decision, but my study leads me to the conclusion that Moses intended to say, as it were, "Not only did Joseph ignore her requests, he avoided being in the same room with her."

That's important. On the one hand, grace-killers will use this reasoning to keep Christians away from all sorts of potential sin—as well as legitimate fun. Take this too far, and you'll become a modern-day Pharisee. On the other hand, be sensible. If something has the power to compromise your integrity at a weak moment, I suggest you avoid it. For instance, if you sense even the slightest attraction to another person's mate or to someone other than your own (if you're married), resolve now to keep your distance and establish some hard-and-fast rules of conduct for yourself. The workbook section to follow this chapter will explain this in more detail.

Despite your best intentions, let's face it, temptation will seek you out. Look at what happened to Joseph.

> Now it happened one day that he went into the house to do his work, and none of the men of the household was there inside. She caught him by his garment,

saying, "Lie with me!" And he left his garment in her hand and fled, and went outside. (Genesis 39:11–12)

The time to resist temptation is *before* we are confronted by it. And when we are, the New Testament commands only one response: RUN! (See 1 Corinthians 6:18; 10:14, 1 Timothy 6:11, and 2 Timothy 2:22.) Don't reason with it, don't argue with it, don't shout Scripture at it, and for heaven's sake, don't start weighing consequences. Run like it's a burning building about to fall in on you, because that word picture is not far from real. You've lost the fight the moment you choose to stand there and fight. Instead, RUN!

Joseph's Reward

Joseph not only fled the room, he ran until he was completely outside the house. William Congreve's words describe her reaction: "Heaven has no rage like love to hatred turned, nor hell a fury like a woman scorned."[6] She wanted Joseph, not his garment. Consequently, Clare Boothe Luce's words equally ring true: "No good deed goes unpunished."

> When she saw that he had left his garment in her hand and had fled outside, she called to the men of her household and said to them, "See, he has brought in a Hebrew to us to make sport of us; he came in to me to lie with me, and I screamed. "When he heard that I raised my voice and screamed, he left his garment beside me and fled and went outside." So she left his garment beside her until his master came home. Then she spoke to him with these words, "The

Hebrew slave, whom you brought to
us, came in to me to make sport of me;
and as I raised my voice and screamed,
he left his garment beside me and fled
outside." (Genesis 39:13–18)

As we read those words, we think, *Oh, if there's ever
a time to reward the man, reward him now, God! Reward
him for answering "no" day after day after day!* But God's
not through with Joseph. God sees a much grander plan
than you or I could have imagined.

Now when his master heard the words
of his wife, which she spoke to him,
saying, "This is what your slave did
to me," his anger burned. So Joseph's
master took him and put him into the
jail, the place where the king's prisoners
were confined; and he was there in the
jail. (Genesis 39:19–20)

Color Joseph confused. He's never read
Genesis 39. He doesn't know what the results will be.
He doesn't know that he will be installed as Prime
Minister of Egypt in a few years. All he knows is that he
did what was right and got this in return. His good was
trumped by evil. I point that out to make the following
point. We can't always expect to receive the rewards of
moral choices right away. More on that later.

But the Lord was with Joseph and
extended kindness to him, and gave
him favor in the sight of the chief jailer.
(Genesis 39:21)

Defeating Temptation

I'm sure that some readers are nodding right now, thinking *Yes! That's good. I need to read this because that's where I stand, and I need this encouragement to keep standing.* Some others are teetering on the fence between right and wrong, and feeling nudged one way or the other as they read. To both I want to offer four "musts" for your consideration. Four different conditions must exist if you are to cultivate a lifestyle of moral purity.

First: You must not allow your circumstances to weaken you. Joseph enjoyed financial security as his master's right-hand man. He was given unprecedented autonomy and privacy because of the trust he had earned. He was strong, handsome, and wise. The security and power of his position mixed with his obvious competence would lead any reasonable person to assume the young man had it made. In truth, though, our position is never as secure as we might hope. Nobody "has it made." I can think of no situation or position that cannot be destroyed in a single day by a moral failure — especially if it's sexual. You must not allow your flesh to delude you into a false sense of security.

Second: You must not reason with temptation. You will lose. Your tempter or temptress will use precisely the words you want to hear. Don't be deceived. Here are some examples:

> "Your husband doesn't meet your needs like I could."

> "By doing this you'll prove that you really care for me."

> "Who will ever find out? We're completely alone, absolutely safe."

"What I'm doing doesn't harm anyone."

"Look, we're going to be married soon anyway."

"I'm so terribly lonely. God understands my need for you."

"Just this once. Never, never, never again."

"Doing the right thing hasn't worked out so far, so God will just have to give me a break."

"What's grace all about if it doesn't leave room for this?"

Those are just some examples. Yours will be tailor-made for you. They look ridiculous in black and white, but when emotions run high and you're feeling safe from detection, they can be amazingly convincing.

Third: You must not coddle your emotions. Without question, they will plead for gentleness and under-standing. They'll get on their knees and beg for mercy, just this once. They'll sweet-talk one minute and sulk the next. But we must be firm. Look at how rugged Joseph was.

In verse 8, "He refused!" In verse 9, he called the words of Potiphar's wife "this great evil, and a sin against God." In verse 10, "he didn't listen to her to lie beside her", or even be in the same room with her. In verse 12, he slipped out of his outer garment in order to flee from her!

Don't be afraid to get downright RUDE about it! The late Dag Hammarskjold wrote in his work, *Markings,* "You cannot play with the animal in you without becoming wholly animal. He who wants to keep his garden tidy doesn't reserve a plot for weeds."[7] Your temptation is not your friend, though it pretends to be. Your temptation hopes to con you out of everything worth anything, so treat it like the enemy it is.

Fourth: You must not be distracted or demoralized by immediate results. Remember David? Nearly a full year went by (perhaps even more) before Nathan put his finger in the great king's face and said, "You are the man!" (2 Samuel 12:7).

Remember Joseph? The sun hadn't gone down on his choice for purity before false accusations filled the house he had served so faithfully. Quite probably the very next day, he found himself in prison for his decision to obey God.

You may be misunderstood or even ridiculed for the stand you take. You may lose your job, even your hope of a great career. One man had a personal standard that he would never travel on business with a woman without at least one other person along. Very wise. But his superiors in the corporation accused him of failing to accept realities of the modern-day workplace. They cajoled him for "not having a mature view of men and women" and for "not having the ability to blind himself to issues of gender" and for "perpetuating negative stereotypes of male-female interaction on the job." No doubt his peculiar stand cost him more than one promotion, but he considered his marriage worth protecting at any cost.

Don't let temporary setbacks keep you from doing what you know to be right. Trust God, even when it doesn't seem to make sense. Trust Him to honor your faith in His time, in His way. Do this and your reward will be far greater than you could ever have imagined. The first lines of verse 21 illustrate the point. "But the Lord was with Joseph and extended kindness to him."

Two Choices, One Destiny

Two great, godly men. Two temptations. Two reactions. Two very different results. David cultivated a lifestyle of sensuality by twisting God's covenant of marriage into a means of indulging himself with a multitude of women. It should come as no surprise that sexual temptation found the middle-aged monarch an easy target. Israel suffered the fallout of his tragic choice for many generations.

Joseph, on the other hand, cultivated a lifestyle of purity. Not surprisingly, the day temptation cast a sensual gaze his way, his disciplined mindset took over, and he fled the scene. True, he suffered Potiphar's unjust punishment, but he continued to receive God's blessing. And because of his obedience, Joseph went from second-in-command in a household to second-in-command over a nation.

Someone once wrote, "Sow a thought, reap an act. Sow an act, reap a habit. Sow a habit, reap your character. Sow your character, reap your destiny." God is sovereign over all, including the future. But He has given you the choice of participating with Him in writing your destiny. As you will see in the study to follow, He has stacked the odds overwhelmingly in favor of your doing right, so that, in the end, you have every advantage and absolutely no excuse.

Choose your destiny well. You'll be in it for a long, long time.

My Questions and Thoughts

_____

_____

_____

_____

_____

_____

_____

_____

_____

_____

_____

_____

_____

_____

_____

_____

_____

_____

_____

_____

_____

_____

_____

_____

_____

My Questions and Thoughts

_____

_____

_____

_____

_____

_____

_____

_____

_____

_____

_____

_____

_____

_____

_____

_____

_____

_____

_____

_____

_____

_____

_____

_____

_____

Chapter 4

You Can Prevail Over Sin

You Are Here

God promised he would rule over his brothers.

When he was a boy, his older brothers looked down on him. And he suffered many difficult years before God's promise proved true. As he ascended from obscurity, he soon found himself endowed with power and responsibility because God was with him.

But when this handsome man faced sexual temptation, *he gave in to it*—and indulged with a woman married to someone else.

Almost sounded like Joseph didn't it? The similarities between David and Joseph seem astounding—up until the end, where the outcomes of their lives are vastly different. Both began in obscurity and rose into prominence through faithfulness to God. Yet unlike David, described above, Joseph *remained* faithful. But how? How did Joseph stay pure while David, a man after God's own heart, gave in to his own sinful urgings?

Think of an example from your own life experience in which two siblings raised in the same Christian (or non-Christian) home had completely different responses to God. What factors do you think contributed to the different outcomes?

Discovering the Way

In our previous study we devoted ourselves to examining 1 Corinthians 10:1–12. There we discovered our security and blessings provide no infallible protection against sin or its consequences. And David's life clearly illustrated this principle. Jonathan Edwards wrote, "They are most safe, who are most sensible of their own weakness; most distrustful of their own hearts; and most sensible of their continual need of restraining grace."[1]

1 Corinthians 10:1–12 warns us of the possibility of falling; verses 13–14 tell us *we don't have to fall.* Joseph's life clearly illustrated this principle.

Begin by circling what you see as the key words in each part of 1 Corinthians 10:13 below. Then record one observation about each phrase.

"No temptation has overtaken you but such as is common to man . . ."

"And God is faithful, who will not allow you to be tempted beyond what you are able . . ."

"But with the temptation [God] will provide the way of escape also, so that you will be able to endure it . . ."

Remember the context of 1 Corinthians 10:13. The specific temptations about which Paul wrote were as "common," or familiar, to the Corinthians as they are to us today: idolatry, sexual immorality, testing God, and grumbling (see verses 7–10). And as the temptations are common today, so are the sins—none are unique to you.

What are the particular temptations that threaten to "overtake" you most often? Be as specific as you can be—time, place, people, things, etc.

In light of your observations of the promises in 1 Corinthians 10:13, why do you think these temptations continue to overtake you?

The text following 1 Corinthians 10:1–12 reveals that we "take heed" first by *believing* something and then by *doing* something. In the next two sections, we'll examine what those are.

What We Should Believe about Temptation

First, we must believe that *temptation is common to every person* (see 1 Corinthians 10:13). Joseph's life proved this to be true.

Read Genesis 39:7–12.

From the following verses in Genesis 39, provide at least one observation about the characteristics of Joseph's *temptations*. Do not include observations about his reactions to these temptations yet.

39:7

39:10

39:11

39:12

What similar aspects of temptation do you and Joseph share? Be specific.

What do you hear the following verses saying about how temptation is "common to man"? Note your observations.

Hebrews 2:18; 4:15

James 1:13–15

1 Peter 5:8–9

Think of a person you know who seems to have it all together. How does it help you in your response to temptation to know that everybody—without exception—faces similar struggles?

How does it help you when you face temptations to know even Jesus suffered under it?

Not only do others struggle with the same temptations as you—yes, even sexual temptation—but God has not left you alone to deal with it apart from Him.

The second thing we need to believe about temptation is that *God is faithful to every believer.* Along with the universal struggle of temptation, Paul revealed God's universal provision to help believers defeat it: His faithfulness (1 Corinthians 10:13).

God demonstrates this faithfulness to every Christian during temptation in two ways. First, *He limits the extent of temptation*—He "will not allow you to be tempted beyond what you are able" (1 Corinthians 10:13).

From the examples below, how does God limit the degree of temptation?

Job 1:10, 12; 2:6

Luke 22:31–32

What do these examples reveal about the seemingly irresistible pull of sexual temptation in your life? Do you believe it is really irresistible?

The second way God shows His faithfulness to us in the midst of temptation is by *providing a way of escape*. With the temptation God "will provide the way of escape also, so that you will be able to endure it" (1 Corinthians 10:13).

Look back at Genesis 39:8–12 and make at least one observation about Joseph's *reactions* to his temptations for each reference below:

39:8

39:9

39:10

39:12

What are the "ways of escape" God provided for Joseph in these verses?

Read Genesis 39:20–21.

What was the *ultimate* "way of escape" from sexual temptation God provided for Joseph according to Genesis 39:20–21?

If you were in a situation like Joseph's, would you see this turn of events as God's provision against temptation? Most of us probably would not. Seeing this experience as coming from God's hand sheds tremendous light on how we should respond to temptation during times of struggle.

If Joseph had grown angry or bitter with God because of his brothers' betrayal (see Genesis 37), how might he have responded differently to the sexual temptations?

In what ways have you rationalized the indulgence of temptation or sexual impurity in the past?

Describe a recent example of how you found a "way of escape" that God provided during temptation.

Later in his story, Joseph revealed his God-given perspective on why God allowed the trials (and temptations) in his life: "You meant evil against me, but God meant it for good to bring about the present result, to preserve many people alive" (Genesis 50:20). The way of escape may not always come as we expect or prefer. But God provides it every single time we face temptation. *This is His promise.*

Getting to the Root

Because God has promised to allow no overwhelming temptation in our lives, we must recognize that our faithfulness comes from what we *choose* in any situation, not from what happens to us. The Bible gives us as sinners a command regarding sin: *repent*. This command is often mistaken to mean simply changing one's actions. But the Greek word for "repent" is *metanoeō*, a compound word literally referring to a "change of mind." [2] This is why Paul first tells the Corinthians *what to believe* and then *what to do*. There can be no true life-change without first a change of mind.

What We Should Do
about Temptation

Having told the Corinthians to *believe something*—namely, that temptation is common and God is faithful—Paul then tells them to *do something*. Notice the simple summary in 1 Corinthians 10:14—"Therefore, my beloved, flee from idolatry." The context that follows verse 14 speaks of ancient idolatry in a specific sense. But the *principle of idolatry* extends to the previous context. In other words, *believing* that temptation is common, and *believing* that God is faithful, what should we therefore *do*? The answer is clear. Take the way of escape—FLEE!

Explain how sexual pleasure, when impure, could be regarded as an idol.

Digging Deeper

"But he refused . . ." (Genesis 39:8). These words illustrate a critical principle we must cling to at moments of temptation: sin remains a choice. First Corinthians 10:13–14 provides the good news that we never face a temptation so strong we cannot resist. But the bad news is that when we sin, we have no excuse. In Romans 6:1–14 Paul provided the liberating truth that because Jesus's death paid the penalty for our sins and we believe in Him, sin's power and authority over us are rendered powerless. "Likewise you also, reckon yourselves to be dead indeed to sin, but alive to God in Christ Jesus our Lord" (Romans 6:11 NKJV). We are no longer slaves to sin. This "dead reckoning" of ourselves frees us to recognize sin as a choice—not a compulsion—and to choose righteousness.

For each verse below, write the dangerous circumstances from which people fled.

Matthew 10:23

Mark 14:50

Acts 7:29

What common element can be found in these circumstances from which people flee — even today?

Now consider that same element in the following verses as you summarize them. (*Danger* is intrinsic to the Greek word for "flee.")

1 Corinthians 6:18

1 Timothy 6:10–11

2 Timothy 2:22

Why do you think believers should have the same fearful response to these things as to the earlier instances of fleeing? Do you think Christians respond to these circumstances in that way? Why or why not?

In addition to the imperative to flee, what action does Paul command Timothy to take in 1 Timothy 6:11 and 2 Timothy 2:22?

One cannot say no to one thing without saying yes to something else more appealing. For believers, that something more appealing is the Lord. The path to sexual purity begins with a pursuit of a deeper relationship with Jesus Christ.

Starting Your Journey

Every destination begins as a journey. Deliberate steps, whether or not the traveler knows the end, determine the direction and ultimately, the destination. Our study so far has revealed the journey to sexual purity comes from a series of daily decisions made with a dual passion: to *flee* and to *pursue.*

To Flee or Not to Flee?

How would you respond if you saw a child playing near a hole where you knew rattlesnakes lived?

Similarly, how ought we to respond to dangerous things that lead to sin in our lives?

Paul's command to "flee" (1 Corinthians 10:14) translates a present imperative in the Greek, indicating something we must *continually* choose to do. "Continue to flee," we could say. Joseph made the decision "day after day . . . not [to] listen to her to lie beside her or be with her" (Genesis 39:10). He chose to flee in a very real sense long before he left his garment in her hands.

Why do you think Joseph refused to "listen to her"?

Why do you think Joseph refused even to "be with her," that is, "be around her"?

Marketers today know that the way a product is presented can stir up our desire to have it. We must never forget that Satan is a great marketer of sin. He often packages sin in such a way that just being exposed to the temptation can hook us unawares. Often we should not only avoid the sin itself, but also those things that could tempt us in an area of weakness.

Jonathan Edwards noted:

> They [people] will not only avoid those things that would be in themselves the ruin of their estates—as setting their own houses on fire, and burning them up with their substance; taking their money and throwing it into the sea, etc.—but they carefully avoid those things by which their estates are exposed. . . .

. . . And therefore, if we are not as careful to avoid sin, as we are to avoid injury in our temporal interest, it will show a regardless disposition with respect to sin and duty; or that we do not much care though we do sin against God. *God's glory is surely of as much importance and concern as our temporal interest. Certainly we should be as careful not to be exposed to sin against the Majesty of heaven and earth, as men are wont to be of a few pounds; yea, the latter are but mere trifles, compared with the former* (emphasis added).[3]

Consider your surroundings. Think about the television, the Internet, a friend of the opposite sex, your work environment, or your gym. What elements of your routine offer sexual temptations of thought, deed, or emotion?

In Homer's *Odyssey*, Ulysses plugged his sailor's ears with wax so that they would not hear the seducing songs of the sirens. And while Ulysses could hear the songs of the temptresses as his ship sailed past, only his being strapped to the mast restrained his madness. Sexual temptation likewise can seem irresistible. And for those who have habitually yielded, sometimes it seems only being tied to a mast can keep them pure.

Consider your surroundings again. What plan of escape do you have in place for times when you hear the "songs of the sirens"?

As odd as it sounds, the time to resist sexual temptation is *before* temptation. You know where and how you've failed before. So set up an impenetrable barrier for yourself. Strap yourself to the mast, if you must! Make it foolproof!

What barrier(s) and plan(s) of escape could you suggest for these areas of temptation?

Internet pornography

Internet chat rooms

A kind or attractive coworker or friend

Fantasy relationships

Any other areas of weakness you've identified

Look back through your strategies. Can you think of a way around these suggestions? If so, go back and make them fail-safe.

When sexual temptation rushes through your heart like adrenaline through the veins, the Bible repeatedly gives one command: FLEE! Literally and physically remove yourself from the temptation—your life depends on it! Remember, Joseph fled without hesitation.

The seventeenth-century pastor John Owen once wrote:

> Rise mightily against *the first actings* of thy distemper, its first conceptions; suffer it not to get the least ground. Do not say, "Thus far it shall go, and no farther." If it have allowance for one step, it will take another. It is impossible to fix bounds to sin. . . . Consider what an unclean thought would have;

it would have thee roll thyself in folly
and filth. Ask *envy* what it would have;
— *murder* and *destruction* is at the end
of it. Set thyself against it with no less
vigour than if it had utterly debased
thee to wickedness. Without this course
thou wilt not prevail. As sin gets ground
in the affections to delight in, it gets also
upon the understanding to slight it.[4]

Remaining "tied to a mast" can keep us from acting
on urges, but it provides a miserable existence. A change
of heart is our ultimate goal. Beyond simply saying no to
sin, we must learn to say yes to God.

Pursue Righteousness

One survey of *Discipleship Journal* readers ranked their
top areas of greatest spiritual challenge. Significantly, 81
percent noted temptations seemed stronger when they
had neglected their time with God. Also, they named
the following as ways they commonly resist temptation: prayer (84 percent), avoidance of compromising
situations (76 percent), Bible study (66 percent), and
personal accountability (52 percent).[5]

**What relationship do you see between spiritual
health and sexual purity?**

**Look at Joseph's own reasons for moral purity in
Genesis 39:9. To what did he appeal?**

How can you appeal to the same source during temptation? Is it realistic to expect yourself to choose faithfulness if your spiritual life is weak?

In a helpful work, *Mortification of Sin in Believers*, John Owen wrote:

> Men are galled with the guilt of a sin that hath prevailed over them; they instantly promise to themselves and God that they will do so no more; they watch over themselves, and pray for a season, until this heat waxes cold, and the sense of sin is worn off: and so mortification goes also, and sin returns to its former dominion. Duties are excellent food for an unhealthy soul; they are no physic for a sick soul. He that turns his meat into his medicine must expect no great operation. . . .
>
> The rage and predominancy of a particular lust is commonly the fruit and issue of a careless, negligent course in general.[6]

The cultivation of sexual purity comes as a by-product of the cultivation of a growing relationship with God. God never intended simply to be our "medicine" but our "meat"—our daily sustenance.

Choose up to five people whose spiritual lives you admire (both men and women) and ask them to candidly answer the following questionnaire about themselves.

Spiritual Growth Questionnaire

1. What is your personal goal for your spiritual life and the biblical basis for the goal?

2. How are you moving toward this goal in your daily life? Specifically:

    • In your personal plan for time in the Word:

    • In your personal plan for time in prayer:

    • In your personal plan for worship:

    • In your personal plan for renewal: (reading, retreats, contact with mentors, times of solitude, etc.)

3. What specific hindrances to your spiritual growth have you encountered? (Examples: pride, sexual temptations, financial pressures, anger, conflict, etc.)

4. What biblical strategies have you developed to overcome these hindrances?

5. Who are the mature believers who hold you accountable in the area of personal spiritual growth? In what specific ways do they hold you accountable?

6. List the five most helpful books you have read in the area of personal spiritual formation or growth in the Christian life.[7]

When you receive answers from those who completed the questionnaire on the previous page, develop a strategy of spiritual growth that works for you. Your personality and needs may differ from theirs, but having a model of successful growth is invaluable. As you plan, check your motives. Are you changing your behavior out of love and devotion to Jesus? Once you've prayerfully charted your course, ask a person or group to help keep you accountable, that you may "pursue righteousness . . . *with those who call on the Lord from a pure heart*" (2 Timothy 2:22, emphasis added).

When we look at the life of Joseph we see a deliberate priority to cultivate purity. Even after Joseph rose to power in a pagan Egypt, he kept only one wife. How was it that Joseph remained pure, but David cratered? Joseph made sexual purity a daily decision.

The good news is this: Your destination can change—even in mid-journey. You may have to stop. You may have to refuel. You may need to let down your pride, ask for directions from a pastor or trusted counselor, or study the map of God's Word. But you can—and must—change directions if you are headed down the path of immorality. Regardless of where you came from and despite what you have done, your journey to sexual purity can begin today. Nothing less than God's glory is at stake, with your own personal freedom and peace of mind as a result.

Will you start your journey today?

My Questions and Thoughts

My Questions and Thoughts

How to Begin a Relationship with God

The Bible is the most marvelous book in the world, and it is the true "life map" that marks the path to God. This map tells us not only how to avoid pitfalls and how to navigate the sudden roadblocks in life, but it also reveals how to enjoy the journey to the fullest. How? It points us to God—our ultimate destination. It tells us how we can come to know God Himself. Let's look at four vital truths the Scripture reveals.

Our Spiritual Condition: Totally Corrupt

The first truth is rather personal. One look in the mirror of Scripture, and our human condition becomes painfully clear:

> There is none righteous, not even one;
> There is none who understands,
> There is none who seeks for God;
> All have turned aside, together they
>   have become useless;
> There is none who does good,
> There is not even one.
> (Romans 3:10–12)

We are all sinners through and through—totally corrupt. Now, that doesn't mean we've committed every atrocity known to humankind. We're not as *bad* as we can be, just as *bad off* as we can be. Sin colors all of our thoughts, motives, words, and actions.

Look around. Everything around us bears the smudge marks of our sinful nature. Despite our best efforts to create a perfect world, crime statistics continue to soar, divorce rates keep climbing, and families keep crumbling.

Something has gone terribly wrong in our society and in ourselves, something deadly. Contrary to how the world would repackage it, "me-first" living doesn't equal rugged individuality and freedom; it equals death. As Paul said in his letter the Romans, "The wages of sin is death" (Romans 6:23)—our emotional and physical death through sin's destructiveness, and our spiritual death resulting from God's righteous judgment of our sin. This brings us to the second truth: God's character.

God's Character: Infinitely Holy

When he observed the condition of the world and the people in it, the wise King Solomon concluded, "Vanity of vanities, all is vanity" (Ecclesiastes 1:2; 12:8). The fact that we know things are not as they should be points us to a standard of goodness beyond ourselves. Our sense of injustice in life "under the sun" implies a perfect standard of justice "above the sun." That standard and source is God Himself. And God's standard of holiness contrasts starkly with our sinful condition.

Scripture says that "God is light, and in Him there is no darkness at all" (1 John 1:5). He is absolutely holy—which creates a problem for us. If He is so pure, how can we who are so impure relate to Him?

Perhaps we could try being better people, try to tilt the balance in favor of our good deeds, or seek out wisdom and knowledge for self-improvement. Throughout history, people have attempted to live up to God's standard by keeping the Ten Commandments or by living by their own code of ethics. Unfortunately, no one can come close to satisfying the demands of God's law. Romans 3:20 says, "By the works of the Law no flesh will be justified in His sight; for through the Law comes the knowledge of sin."

Our Need: A Substitute

So here we are, sinners by nature, sinners by choice, trying to pull ourselves up by our own bootstraps and attain a relationship with our holy Creator. But every time we try, we fall flat on our faces. We can't live a good enough life to make up for our sin because God's standard isn't "good enough"—it's perfection. And we can't make amends for the offense our sin has created.

Who can get us out of this mess?

If someone could live perfectly, honoring God's law, and would bear sin's death penalty for us—in our place—then we would be saved from our predicament. But is there such a person? Thankfully, yes!

Meet your substitute—*Jesus Christ*. He is the One who took death's place for you!

> [God] made [Jesus Christ] who knew no sin to be sin on our behalf, that we might become the righteousness of God in Him.
> (2 Corinthians 5:21)

God's Provision: A Savior

God rescued us by sending His Son, Jesus, to die for our sins on the cross (see 1 John 4:9–10). Jesus was fully human and fully divine (John 1:1, 18), a truth that ensures His understanding of our weaknesses, His power to forgive, and His ability to bridge the gap between God and us (see Romans 5:6–11). In short, we are "justified as a gift by His grace through the redemption which is in Christ Jesus" (Romans 3:24). Two words in this verse bear further explanation: *justified* and *redemption*.

Justification is God's act of mercy, in which He declares believing sinners righteous, while they are still in their sinning state. Justification doesn't mean that God *makes* us righteous so that we never sin again, rather that He *declares* us righteous—much like a judge pardons a guilty criminal. Because Jesus took our sin upon Himself and suffered our judgment on the cross, God forgives our debt and proclaims us PARDONED.

Redemption is God's act of paying the ransom price to release us from our bondage to sin. Held hostage by Satan, we were shackled by the iron chains of sin and death. Like a loving parent whose child has been kidnapped, God willingly paid the ransom for you. And what a price He paid! He gave His only Son to bear our sins—past, present, and future. Jesus's death and resurrection broke our chains and set us free to become children of God (see Romans 6:16–18, 22; Galatians 4:4–7).

Placing Your Faith in Christ

These four truths describe how God has provided a way to Himself through Jesus Christ. Since the price has been paid in full by God, we must respond to His free gift of eternal life in total faith and confidence in Him to save us. We must step forward into the relationship with God that He has prepared for us—not by doing good works or being a good person, but by coming to Him just as we are and accepting His justification and redemption by faith.

> For by grace you have been saved
> through faith; and that not of your-
> selves, it is the gift of God; not as a
> result of works, that no one should
> boast. (Ephesians 2:8–9)

We accept God's gift of salvation simply by placing our faith in Christ alone for the forgiveness of our sins. Would you like to enter a relationship with your Creator by trusting in Christ as your Savior? If so, here's a simple prayer you can use to express your faith:

Dear God,

I know that my sin has put a barrier between You and me. Thank You for sending Your Son, Jesus, to die in my place. I trust in Jesus alone to forgive my sins, and I accept His gift of eternal life. I ask Jesus to be my personal Savior and the Lord of my life. Thank You. In Jesus's name I pray, Amen.

If you've prayed this prayer or one like it and you wish to find out more about knowing God and His plan for you in the Bible, contact us at Insight for Living. You can speak to one of our pastors or women's counselors on staff by calling or you may send a letter to the address listed in the We Are Here for You section on page 101.

The next time you study a road map, remember the One who created the perfect plan for your life, and remind yourself that you know Him personally. Rejoice in His indescribable gift!

$\mathcal{E}$ndnotes

OPENING QUOTE

1. Alister E. McGrath, *The Journey: A Pilgrim in the Lands of the Spirit*, 1st ed. (New York: Doubleday, 2000), 21–22.

WELCOME TO *LIFEMAPS*

1. Jonathan Edwards, *The Works of Jonathan Edwards,* ed. Edward Hickman, vol. 2 (Carlisle, Penn.: Banner of Truth Trust, 1992), 246.

CHAPTER 1

1. G. Frederick Owen, *Abraham to the Middle East Crisis*, 4th ed., revised (Grand Rapids, Mich.: William B. Eerdmans Publication Co., 1957), 51.

2. Dietrich Bonhoeffer, *Creation and Fall/Temptation: Two Biblical Studies* (New York: Touchstone, 1997), 132.

3. Raymond Brown, *Skillful Hands: Studies in the Life of David* (Fort Washington, Penn.: Christian Literature Crusade, 1972), 99.

4. Thomas Baird, *Conscience* (New York: Charles C. Cook, 1914), 24.

5. James Dobson, *Love Must Be Tough*, (Waco, TX: Word Books, 1983), 135.

6. Randy Alcorn, "Consequences of a Moral Tumble," *Leadership*, vol. 9, issue 1, Winter, 1988, 46. Related articles may be found at www.epm.org.

CHAPTER 2

1. From Sheldon Vanauken, "The Loves," from *Under the Mercy*, as quoted by Chuck Colson, "Why Christians Divorce: The Sanction of Eros," *BreakPoint* radio broadcast, February 17, 2000, © 2000, Prison Fellowship, P.O. Box 17500, Washington, DC, 20041-0500.

2. Shirley P. Glass, *NOT "Just Friends": Rebuilding Trust and Recovering Your Sanity After Infidelity*, paperback ed. (New York: Free Press, 2004), 3.

3. Steve Farrar, *Finishing Strong: Going the Distance for Your Family* (Sisters, Ore.: Multnomah Books, 1995), 27–28.

4. Benedict Carey, "The Roots of Temptation," *Los Angeles Times*, October 20, 2003, sec. F.

5. Walter Bauer, and others, *A Greek-English Lexicon of the New Testament and Other Early Christian Literature*, 2d rev. ed. (Chicago: University of Chicago Press, 1979), 201–202.

6. Charles Haddon Spurgeon, *Morning and Evening* (Grand Rapids, Mich: Zondervan, 1955), 153.

CHAPTER 3

1. Dietrich Bonhoeffer, *Creation and Fall/Temptation: Two Biblical Studies* (New York: Touchstone, 1997), 132.

2. F.B. Meyer, *Joseph: Beloved—Hated—Exalted* (London: Morgan and Scott, Ltd., 1910), 35.

3. Thomas Carlyle, *On Heroes, Hero-Worship, and the Heroic in History* (New York: F.A. Stokes & Brother, 1888), 215.

4. Clarence Edward Macartney, *Trials of Great Men of the Bible* (New York: Abingdon-Cokesbury Press, 1946), 46.

5. Macartney, *Trials of Great Men of the Bible*, 47.

6. William Congreve, *The Mourning Bride, Poems, and Miscellanie* (London: Oxford University Press, 1928), 125.

7. Dag Hammarskjold, *Markings* (New York: Alfred A. Knopf, 1966), 15.

CHAPTER 4

1. Jonathan Edwards, *The Works of Jonathan Edwards*, ed. Edward Hickman, vol. 2 (Carlisle, Penn.: Banner of Truth Trust, 1992), 231.

2. W.E. Vine, and others, *Vine's Expository Dictionary of Biblical Words* (Nashville: Thomas Nelson Publishers, 1985), 525.

3. Edwards, *The Works of Jonathan Edwards*, 228.

4. John Owen, *The Works of John Owen*, ed. William H. Goold, vol. 6 (Carlisle, Penn.: Banner of Truth Trust, 2000), 62.

5. "DJ Readers Report" in "Temptation: Fighting to Win," *Discipleship Journal* 12, no. 6 (November/December 1992), 42.

6. Owen, *The Works of John Owen*, 18, 42.

7. Spiritual Growth Questionnaire was developed by Dr. David B. Wyrtzen, Senior Pastor of Midlothian Bible Church, Midlothian, Texas.

We Are Here for You

We designed this volume of *LifeMaps* to help you on a journey of lasting life-change. Along the way, you may need further insight, encouragement, or simply prayer with a fellow traveler. Insight for Living provides staff pastors and women's counselors who are available for free written correspondence or phone consultation. These seminary-trained men and women have years of pastoral experience and are well-qualified guides for your spiritual journey.

Please feel welcome to contact our Pastoral Ministries Department by calling the Insight for Living Care Line: (972) 473-5097, 8 A.M. through 5 P.M. Central Time. Or you may write to the following address:

Insight for Living
Pastoral Ministries Department
Post Office Box 269000
Plano, Texas 75204

Ordering Information

Cultivating Purity in an Impure World

If you would like to order additional *LifeMaps*, purchase the audio series that accompanies this workbook, or request our product catalog, please contact the office that serves you.

United States and International Locations:

Insight for Living
Post Office Box 269000
Plano, Texas 75026-9000
1-800-772-8888, 24 hours a day, seven days a week
(U.S. contacts)
International constituents may contact the U.S. office through mail queries or call 1-972-473-5136.
www.insight.org

Canada:

Insight for Living Ministries
Post Office Box 2510
Vancouver, BC V6B 3W7
1-800-663-7639
www.insightforliving.ca

Australia and South Pacific:

Insight for Living, Inc.
Post Office Box 1011
Bayswater, VIC 3153
AUSTRALIA
Toll-free 1300 467 444
www.insight.asn.au